Change For Health

Making positive changes in your life and in your
health through Ericksonian principles.

By

M. Eugene Morgan

Editec
by

I0157821

Joseph D. Ramsey

Published by

Nagrome, LLC

Nagrome, LLC

1151 Freeport Road
Suite #369
Pittsburgh, PA 15238
email address: meu_mor@msn.com
Website: www.ChangeForHealth.com

Change For Health

ISBN 978-0-9916191-0-8

Table of Contents

Acknowledgement

Thank you Ronald A. Havens for your commentary and editorial work on Volume I and II of the Wisdom of Milton H. Erickson and the many quotes you've compiled. These two books have saved me many hours of searching for and developing a basic framework for understanding Dr. Erickson's work. Most of all, Dr. Erickson who has given me so much from his work. He has inspired me to be me.

Preface

This book is based on the work of Dr. Milton Erickson; it is compiled from messages in my blog, www.changeforhealth.com, begun in 2009. In two years of blogging, quite a number of blog posts have accumulated, on a wide variety of principles, such as learning, the conscious and unconscious mind, acceptance, celebration of life, and what Dr. Erickson calls our "storehouse of knowledge" to assist us in difficult times. These posts range in length from 300 to 1000 words.

In June 2011, I got the idea of writing briefer messages. Also, I noticed over the years reading Dr. Erickson's work that he often left an idea or two with his subjects, students, and patients, to inspire them and evoke responses from them. I decided to write each day of the week, Monday through Friday, to the same end—to inspire, evoke, and laugh, with Ericksonian principles.

Having accumulated quite a number of messages, I thought it would be good to organize a number of them into the form of a book—this book—to inspire people. When I read back the material, I still find myself inspired by the Ericksonian point of view and hope you are too.

Domesticated Camel

While traveling through a desert, an old man spotted a tamed camel. "My master abandoned me," the camel cried; "I won't survive the desert." After hearing this, the old man took his saddle off the camel he was riding on and then placed it on the abandoned camel's back. "What are you doing," the camel asked. The old man replied, "You say you don't have a master? I'll be your master." "But you're deserting your own camel," the domesticated camel stated. The old man said, "No, I don't own this camel."

The old man jumped on the camel's back and yelled, "Go towards the sun!" After traveling a ways the old man cried, "I'm thirsty! Would you like a drink of water?" "I'm not thirsty," the camel answered. So the old man took a drink. After a while the old man said, "I'm thirsty! Would you like some water?" Again, the camel said, "No!" So the old man took another drink of water.

Later, the camel and the old man had dinner and called it a night. The temperature began dropping. The old man was asleep when his trembled body had awakened him from the bitter cold. "My fur keeps me warm on cold nights

Domesticated Camel

like this," the camel said, "If you like, you can lie next to me." The old man took his offer.

After a sound sleep, the early morning sun had awakened the camel and the old man. "You would have found me dead but because of your warm fur I am alive. Thank you." Just after they were about to continue on west, a desert sandstorm erupted. What was in front of him, the old man could no longer see but the sand storm. "Get behind me!" the camel yelled. "That way you will be protected. My long eyelashes and ear hairs will protect me from the sandstorm." The old man was very grateful for this and thanked the camel.

After a long journey, the old man said, "I have reached my destination." He took his saddle off the camel's back. "Are you deserting me too?" asked the camel. "I've saved your life!" the camel cried. "The desert heat, the desert cold, the desert sandstorm—these are events from which you've saved me," the old man replied, "so you don't need a master. The master of the desert is you, not me."

Written By M. Eugene Morgan

Chapter 1 Abilities

I win Olympic Championships

"Out of a wheelchair I win Olympic championships all the time." — Milton Erickson[1]

As you can see from Erickson's quote, he's good at turning a phrase. It's interesting how he links "a wheelchair" with winning "Olympic championships" together.

The message he wants us to get is that in spite of our limitations, we don't have to yield to them. Erickson made himself an example for people around him that he set goals and carry them out even in a wheelchair.

All of us have different kinds of limitations that get in the way of our goals. Erickson wants us to stop looking at our limitations, and start looking toward our goals we set and win championships.

It's also interesting that Erickson didn't say he won the state, national, or international championships, he said Olympic championships. In other words, he's saying be unafraid to go for the big win—go for the gold!

Pretend and Master It

"You can pretend anything and master it."
—Milton Erickson[2]

When we were kids, we did much pretending. Pretending was the first part of becoming what we wished to become. When we pretended being somebody, we took on the mindset of the person we wished to become.

A child feels a lot safer without judgments or consequences. Pretending fulfills a childhood fantasy. As children, we knew that pretending was just an imaginary game; we had fun doing it.

Erickson says we cannot only pretend being a thing but we can master it. If we pretend being or doing the same thing enough times, then we can eventually master it.

Let's Show Compassion by Using our Talents

We ought to take pride in our abilities to make changes in our lives. We shouldn't let others get us down when we're trying to make it in life.

Instead, we ought to listen to our inner voice, being realistic in what we can do and content in what we already have.

We all have different talents. Talents are contributors to making the world a better place.

Some of us aren't using our talents enough to effect changes in our lives and to help others around us.

Let us use more of our abilities to aid others in need. Compassion is a nice virtue; it can change us from the inside.

Certainties & Uncertainties

"If you are uncertain about yourself, you can't be certain about anything else." — Milton Erickson[3]

In other words, we ought to believe in ourselves. No one knows us better than we know ourselves.

Erickson would take it further to say that our unconscious mind knows us better than we know ourselves consciously.

Erickson is also saying in the above quote, that certainty starts with us first. Until we work on ourselves, we can't be certain about anything else in life.

Our fears can create uncertainties in our minds while courage can create certainties in our minds.

Fear without action is doubt, while fear with action is courage. The energy of fear can fuel the action of courage.

Trusting Our Abilities

All our abilities were once learned. When we take our abilities for granted, we forget that it took hard work for us to acquire our abilities.

We forget that it took time for us to acquire new abilities, but we have many abilities, such as walking, driving, running, riding a bike, writing, reading, etc.

When we want to learn a new skill, we want to learn it quickly. We get impatient with ourselves because we want to learn a new skill well as our previous skills in a short period.

But, when we are impatient we wait twice as long than if we were patient. In other words, we don't have to rush learning. It's better to learn the basics and not to skip ahead, because we might miss something we need to know before continuing to the next level.

Our Own Abilities

When we begin to doubt our own abilities, there is some conscious interference. It is easier to doubt our own abilities and not believe. Because with doubt, we don't attempt to use our own abilities, when they're needed.

When working with a subject, one of Milton Erickson's goals was to discharge doubts in a variety of ways, because doubts interfere with progress. There will come a time when our abilities are tested.

When that time comes, we acknowledge that we can only do so much and that we have given it our best. This doesn't mean we're giving up on our abilities or we're giving into our doubts; it means we find another way to make progress.

Improve Your Time

Improvement is a gift from time. To fine-tune a skill, we must use it daily. If we want to develop a new skill, we must take every opportunity to practice honing the skill, and this requires time well spent.

If we want to become an expert at our skill, we must practice and practice more. If we want to get better or improve on a skill, then we must use it.

Textbooks won't help us become better runners. We must go out and run to become better. But if we want to train for marathon, we must start with small runs first and then work ourselves up to a marathon run.

After running our first marathon, then we can train to beat our personal time. We never stop improving on things.

Better To Do Something, Than Not

The fear of failure is looking at what we can't do instead of looking at what we can do. It keeps us from going beyond what is possible.

If we think a certain way that's not conducive to what we want to carry out, then we will fail. The fear of failure is a belief that it's impossible to do something new and therefore we won't even try.

A change of attitude is in order. Why not accept that failure is possible since we won't get it perfectly on our first try. The imperfections are just to help us to see what we need to improve.

When we switch to this mindset, then the anxiety of failure will decrease. The fear of failure has no value but improvement does.

Relying On Our Abilities

If we want to make progress in our lives, we must believe in ourselves. Relying on our abilities is the main ingredient for success. When we don't believe in ourselves then no progress is possible.

We all have certain levels of confidence in ourselves. When it comes to certain things that challenge us, we become uncertain about our abilities.

But once we begin to feel confidence in our new abilities, we begin to rely more on ourselves. Self-reliance is the inner attitude that we have that says to ourselves that we are certain that we will get things done.

Abilities

The Basic Form Of Creativity is Work

The most valuable asset that any one of us can have is our ability to work. Working builds self-esteem and develops camaraderie among co-workers.

Almost everything that's living does some form of work. Work asks for our undivided attention. Learning is always constant when working.

Work does not necessarily mean working for a company. Cutting grass or running a vacuum cleaner is work as well. To work means to focus mentally or physically to do something to produce results.

Work is a byproduct of creativity. We all experience thinking of a solution only later to find a solution to a problem while working on something else.

To work is a gift, because when we work, we use all our senses. When we use our senses, we experience things around us.

Work is hard. Work helps us to exercise our abilities. Work helps us to stretch when we don't want to. Work helps us to stay patient when we don't want to. Work helps us to stay disciplined when we don't want to. Working builds character.

Abilities

What's Our Purpose?

We don't necessarily need to know why we're here. Instead, we need to find our purpose and then pursue it.

How do we find out what our purpose is? One way is to know our talents.

We all have different types of talents, which makes us unique. We can use our talents to contribute to society in our own unique way. Using our talent is about self-discovery and being ourselves. Most of us know what our talents are.

If we don't know what our talents are, we can find out. We've all experienced someone complimenting us on the way we do certain things. We've all noticed that the same compliments are not always from the same person but from array of different people.

Receiving compliments on the same thing from different people should be our big clue, if we don't know what our talents are.

For some reason, some of us want to avoid pursuing or developing one of our talents. And that's okay because we each have more than one to pursue.

Chapter 2 Conscious and Unconscious Mind

Trusting Our Intuition

Trusting our intuition means trusting our unconscious mind. We always see things clearly after an event has happened. But if we trust our instincts or intuition some problems can be avoided.

We can learn to trust our intuition. We must train ourselves to pay attention to what we feel. Our unconscious minds can pick up things that we don't notice consciously.

It give us clues like a feeling, or an internal voice telling us something. These clues can aid us in making decision, keeping us out of danger, and being an effective communicator.

In short our intuition can see things far beyond the scope of our conscious mind.

When it's Time to Wonder

It is time to wonder, when we can't come up with an idea. It is time to wonder, when we have fewer choices. It is time to wonder, when we're on the verge of making an important decision.

It is time to wonder, when we need to see beyond ourselves. It is time to wonder, when we have no clue on what step is next. It is time to wonder, when we don't have answers for life's mysteries.

Milton Erickson used to encourage his subjects to wonder. Wondering is distracting the conscious mind away from immediate reality, allowing our unconscious part of us to emerge.

When more of the unconscious mind emerges, more options and more creativity surfaces to help with personal changes in our lives.

Meet Me In Your Dream's Garden

January 9, 2012, was the second anniversary of my father's passing. I still miss him. If I just look in the mirror, I see him.

Whenever I think of him, I feel him in my heart. My unconscious mind has learned every pattern of sounds he had made, every pattern of movements he had made, and so I can talk with him in my dreams.

As far as I know, I haven't met him in my dreams. Perhaps I don't need to. But when I do need to talk, I will meet him there.

One thing that's so powerful about our unconscious mind is that it will continue to search for the experiences that we all have had with our lost loved-ones that we can continue to feel them, long after we've stopped thinking about them, as though they're still alive.

Resolving a Problem Consciously or Unconsciously

When we find ourselves with nagging thoughts, it is usually from something that hasn't been resolved within us. We replay a tape of an event that happened six hours ago. As we replay these tapes, we re-injure ourselves emotionally.

We can no longer blame the external event or even ourselves for that matter because it's something that we can't help. This process is consciously learned, then the learning becomes unconscious.

But to unlearn this process, it must become conscious again, then we can learn a healthier way to deal with the event that causes raw and hurtful feelings. This is one way of resolving this problem.

However, Milton Erickson trusts the un-conscious mind to help to resolve problems. Erickson gets the subject to experience things directly to help break up rigid frames that are causing the problem.

Finding a Solution

Sometimes we don't have the answers we're looking for within us; that's because we haven't experienced them yet.

Neither our conscious mind nor our unconscious mind has learned how yet. This means we need to look outside ourselves to look for what we need to learn to find a solution.

We may be thinking of the situation in too vague a way to really find them. Once we learn to turn a vague situation into something specific, then we can be free from the traps and see clearly what needs to be changed.

The Recipes of Our Live

Milton Erickson says that we have a storehouse of learning and experiences in our unconscious mind. Our unconscious mind is like a storehouse of groceries where we have shopped, and where we have bought the usual items every week.

Sometimes we have a new recipe we want to try. If it's a grocery store we shop regularly, we can generally find most of the ingredients we need.

However, there are times when we have difficulty finding an ingredient for a recipe. This forces us to search in other areas of the store we don't normally shop.

We have to make sure we get the right sizes and kinds of items. Sometimes the store maybe out of something, and we may need to do without or find a substitute. All of this takes time.

In such a way, we can use our unconscious mind's storehouse to help us through the recipes of life.

A Spontaneous Laugh!

When was the last time we had a good laugh? A good laugh is good for the mind, the body and the soul, because it's better to let things go than to hold on to things.

When we hear the first part of a joke, we're expecting a foregone conclusion. However, when we hear the second part of the joke (the punch line), it's unexpected and it triggers pleasure in the brain.

When we look at it with the conscious and the unconscious mind, the first part of the joke we hear consciously and the second part of the joke, there is an unconscious search.

The unconscious mind searches for meaning and understanding of the punch line. So when we get the joke, we laugh. It's truly a spontaneous laugh!

Understanding More through Our Unconscious mind

"And we can understand more than we think we can." — Milton Erickson[4]

In the above quote, Erickson is suggesting to the subjects to open up the door of storehouse of their unconscious mind. Sometimes we quickly dismiss the things we don't understand. We try to understand things with our conscious mind and not with our unconscious mind.

Remember, our unconscious mind is constantly at work learning new things that we're unaware of. Only a small fraction of learning is from our conscious mind and then it's transferred to our unconscious mind.

Erickson always separate the two entities; the unconscious and conscious mind because there are two different types of thinking. The conscious mind is rigid and makes assumptions about things whereas unconscious mind is flexible and observant about things.

"As A Man Thinketh, He Is, or Dreams He Is"

"And philosophers of old have said, "As a man thinketh, he is." — Milton Erickson[5]

Erickson is saying in the above quote, that we have the ability to think whatever we want in our minds. Whatever occupying thoughts we attend to, are what we are. Erickson is always interested in getting a subject to experience thinking, because thinking creates feeling and feeling creates action. Erickson's goal is action.

Sometimes, we may feel an emotion and not know why. These are unaware thoughts that create the emotions within us. These unaware thoughts are detached from our conscious mind because our unconscious mind protects our conscious mind.

And the unaware thoughts are usually played out in our dreams for us to experience.

Erickson believes that to experience something means to start the change from within. He uses the internal resources (the dream stuff) that we have in the storehouses of our unconscious mind to help effect change.

Feeling is Essential

"The feeling is the essential thing. Knowing about it is not the essential thing."
— Milton Erickson[6]

Let us feel our emotions. In our daily lives, our unconscious minds tells us what we're feeling. In the above quote Erickson believed it's important to experience our feelings instead of analyzing them.

We can't think our feelings through but we can feel our feelings through. When our unconscious mind tell us that we're thirsty we normally don't think about why we're thirsty, instead; we go and get something to drink to fulfill the need.

In the same way, with our feelings we simply need to express them so we can replenish our self-respect, that's why feeling is the essential thing. Hostility increases when our self-respect depletes. Feelings are energy in motion. They have to go somewhere; we can't keep them inside.

Leaving The Past Behind Us

"And the unpleasantnesses and unhappinesses of the past–leave them in the past, way back in the past." — Milton Erickson[7]

Are there any benefits of bringing up the past? When we bring up our painful past into the present we stop living in the present and stop looking ahead towards the future.

The past becomes the lens of our present and future. We see no hope for our future when we stay stranded in the past. Looking back at the past is just an extra weight we don't need.

It's too difficult to walk towards the future when we are carrying the weight of the past with us. Letting go of the past isn't an easy thing to do. Some of us have an intimate relationship with our unhappy and unpleasant past. Some of us are emotionally invested and can't or won't let go. Nonetheless, we can start to look ahead. It's our choice.

Chapter 3 Efforts

Challenge Calls For Action

When we experience boredom, it could mean that we're not challenging ourselves enough. When we challenge ourselves to do something that goes against every fiber of our being, we are stimulating growth.

When we're challenging ourselves, we're calling for action. Challenging ourselves arouses action and interest in what we want to do. One of the reasons we like a challenge is that we want to see if we can do it.

Making a challenge out of whatever we do can help motivate us to begin and to stay with it until completion.

It's a real joy when we see that we can carry out something in spite of the amount of difficulties it may bring. A challenge means never giving up and remaining true to ourselves.

Challenging means to make an honest effort to ourselves and then to others who are cheering us on to get through it. It's about competing with ourselves.

Persistence Through Life's Difficulties

In spite of our fears and doubts, we must persist in what we're trying to carry out. We may lose some things while being persistent, but if we lose persistence itself, then everything is lost.

Persistence means continuing in spite of difficulties. Difficulties are there to fine–tune and make us stronger, but they're not easy to face.

It takes a lot of energy to keep up persistence. In spite of our feelings, it pushes us up the hill. We must keep moving, though it's all right to take a break or two. We're going to need them to climb a steep hill.

We will always have difficulties ahead. Instead of the avoiding them, we can face them, if we persist.

Inspiration Motivates Success

We don't have to feel overwhelmed or feel envious when we see someone's success. Instead, we can be inspired by the person's successes and achievements.

We can see that if they can succeed then we can succeed as well. It's more inspiring when we see their success; they've proven to us that it is possible to succeed. Such inspiration is the juice that motivates us to put in the hard work and the show the willingness to go beyond the call of duty.

When we're ready to sacrifice, we're giving ourselves permission to do what it takes to get where we want to go. It's really a decision we have to make for ourselves.

Being indecisive will only drag us down. It's hard to do our best when we're indecisive. It implies that we haven't really made our minds up.

Once we've made our minds up to do what we want, a possibility emerges that we will carry out our goals. We just need to get inspired and do it.

Mini Goals: The End In Sight

If we work now, our efforts will pay off later. It's important to make an effort in everything we do to obtain our goals. Today we make the effort, tomorrow or several months or even a year from now we will reap the rewards.

Since it's going to take time to see our efforts pay off, we ought to develop contingency plan. We can start turning our long-term goals into mini goals.

With mini goals, we can see the end in sight. Completing a mini goal is a reward in itself. The reward will encourage us to go to the next mini goal. It is simply a lot easier to complete mini goals than it is to complete long-term goals.

A Fulfilled Dream Requires a Commitment

When committed to something, there is no indecision, there are no ambiguities, there are no distractions, and there are no excuses. We just do what is required of us.

It's nice to have a fantasy about doing something that will better our situation. But bringing our vision into reality is a serious business.

We let ourselves down when we don't take it seriously. For example, when we say we'll do something and then don't do it, we're disappointing ourselves, and more self-doubt begins to creep in.

Part of the process of fulfilling our vision is to do the many tasks to get our vision to the foreground. Although it requires one step to start the thousand-mile journey, it also requires a commitment to finish it.

Commitment requires the body, mind, and spirit to align to bring a vision into reality.

The Long Way Is the Shorter Way

When it comes to hard work or completing a difficult task, there is always the temptation of making shortcuts. Some shortcuts can be useful, but shortcuts can be more bothersome than they're worth.

For example, there are some things we have to learn before we go ahead on a project. And learning takes time, time that most of us don't have.

If we make learning a valuable commodity to completing a task, then it's better to make the time to learn how to continue. Besides, learning to do something correctly will save us time in the long run.

Anticipating Obstacles

When things aren't going our way, patience is required. Just like a deadline we have to meet, things won't always go smoothly as planned.

We must expect setbacks and accept them as they occur. Our goal is to get through obstacles, one obstacle at a time.

Obstacles will delay us, and that's their function, to delay our progress, but they will always be around as long as we move from point A to point B.

Obstacles shouldn't stop us from meeting our goals. Obstacles are opposing forces that only slow our progress, and that's all. We needn't give up on our goals because of obstacles.

Inspiration is Deceptive

"What it boils down to is one percent inspiration and ninety-nine percent perspiration."
— Thomas Edison[8]

When we come up with a great idea that inspires us, it takes much work to bring the idea into fruition. Inspiration moves us to begin to do something, but the rest, as Thomas Edison suggests, takes work.

That's the difference between someone who's willing to learn and do the work and someone who stays idle. If we want something to happen, we must do the work to make it happen.

We will fall while doing it, but we have the strength and the ability to get back up. Inspiration is the energy in motion to give us a head start.

Complete it, Your reward will be Satisfying

We can't always complete things in one day. There will always be another day to complete a task. However, some things need completion.

It depends on what it is we need completed. Deadlines require us to complete the task. However, some deadlines don't need completion on the same day; the task is due on a certain day but not today.

It's better to start on a task now than to wait as the deadline gets closer. Nonetheless, some of us work better under pressure when a deadline is approaching.

There is also tension in our body to finish something. That tension or pressure compels us to complete the task. We don't want anything hanging over our heads. After completion, we are rewarded by a feeling of satisfaction.

When it begins to Feel Right

When things begin to feel right, we know it's a good thing we're doing. The hard work is beginning to pay off; we begin to see progress.

Progress is a slow process. It takes time to see it, but it's there. This is why we ought to start now without delay. Time is ticking. Time doesn't wait on anyone, and we can never get it back.

But when we do start up a project and work on it daily, time flies when we're having fun. And at the end of the year we can look and see how much we have accomplished.

Most of us would rather have done something and look back to see progress than look back and see nothing but regrets. So let's do something now and feel right about doing it later.

Breaking down the Barriers through Discipline

What barriers do we have that keep us from making changes in our lives? Fears, excuses, distractions, just to name a few, can keep us from the real changes we want.

Doubting is a mental exercise that creates fear in the body. We need our bodies in action to make changes. Excuses are another way of avoiding change, because we don't know where that change will take us. Distraction is just keeping us occupied on aimless things.

We've all heard that it takes 30 days to break a habit and it also takes 30 days to learn a new habit. There is a nasty word called 'discipline.' For some of us the word 'discipline' conjures up punishment and order.

However, discipline can be associated with the words like 'focus' and 'concentration' for a certain amount time to begin, to keep up and to finish a task. The task is one of many to gradually assist changes in one's life.

Discipline can keep our fears, excuses and distractions at bay. Discipline can help us keep our eyes on the ball.

Self-discovery

"The person that has the most to do with what happens to you is you. It's not somebody else."
— Dr. Ben Carson[9]

This quote falls in line with Milton Erickson's view that we have the power within ourselves to improve our situation, if we choose to.

We have it within our control to succeed if we put in the labor that is necessary to get there. Once we realize that we make the most of what happens to us, we can direct our energy and align our mind, body and soul to what we want in life.

There is freedom in knowing that we can control our path to where we want to go in our lives. There is no freedom in blaming external realities. Blaming external realities only keeps us prisoners in our self-denial. Instead, let us get out of self-denial and into self-discovery.

Enjoy in the Process

"We learn our goals only in the process of getting there." — Milton Erickson[10]

When setting our goals we tend to look at the
product, instead of enjoying the process itself.
Part of the process is about learning something
new. There is something about learning new
things that enriches our lives and keeps things
refreshing—and, completing our goals is just the
icing on the cake. The truth is, the process can
get painful at times. But it's the struggle that
makes us stronger in the long run and makes
that icing on the cake sweeter at the end. The
process changes us for the better. It makes us
better people.

The Answers Within

"I don't need to know what your problem is for you to correct it." — Milton Erickson[11]

Erickson is saying in the above quote that we have it in ourselves to correct our problems. Sometimes, we just need someone to steer us in the right direction. The answers are within each of us. We just need to learn how to get access to them. It's just that sometimes, we don't listen to our inner voice that's telling us the answers. Erickson is also saying that it's our responsibility to correct our own problems. No one can really correct our problems for us. It's about changing our perspective on our reality.

Leaving it to Effort

Putting in the effort does a lot to our psyches. When we put an earnest effort into a particular task, we feel good about ourselves. The good feeling creates a psychological effect and reinforces our efforts.

Starting something new is the hardest thing to do, but then it gets easier as we put in the daily effort. Part of the difficulty of putting in the effort is that we want quick results, but quick results will not always ensue.

We will always get something out of our efforts. The most important thing we will get out of our efforts is experience.

Experience is a collection of our efforts. It is a resource to help us to expand our view.

Chapter 4 Goals

Desire to Meet Life's Goals

We all have desires to meet life's goals. There are some goals that are left undone. Unmet goals yield feelings of regret; regrets only remind us of our incomplete projects, our procrastination, our idleness, and our indecision.

But to meet our life's goals, we must learn to complete things. We can start by completing small projects that are manageable. Milton Erickson says we're simple creatures, therefore we should keep projects as simple as we can.

Sometimes, we have too many goals or projects and we end up getting lost in the distraction, unfocused on completing things. Doing one project at a time keeps our undivided attention on nothing but the project that's in front of us.

We live in a culture that wants things done quickly. But if we take the time in the beginning, we can save time later.

Goals

Plan a Change

It's up to us to make a change.   We have the power within ourselves to make a change, if we want to.   If we want to improve our lives, we then have to decide to improve it.   After we decide to improve our situation, we then can write up a plan.   After a plan is in place, we then can execute the plan until it's completed.

No other person can make the change for us.   In other words, relying on someone to make a change is useless; it won't ever happen.   When we rely on someone, we are giving away our power.   Ultimately, we know what we want in life so it's better to ask ourselves, "What do I want for my life?" and we then can make a plan and execute it, because within us we have the power.

"If you want it you must obtain it by great labor." — T.S. Eliot[22]

Why Goals

Sometimes we give up too soon on a dream or a goal, because it seems so big or we worry about what others may think. It's easier to come up with excuses than to trek through the goals we set for ourselves.

Sometimes, we doubt ourselves way before we start working on the goal. But goals are opportunities for personal growth. Goals are deliberate. Goals awaken our potentials. Goals are rewarding when completed.

There are short-term goals and long-term goals. Long-term goals are mini short-term goals met steadily. Meeting short-term goals is like connecting another piece of train track for the wheel of a cart to move forward. It sounds tedious, because part of work will be tedious, but it's necessary.

Start Today, Not Tomorrow

Procrastination likes to eat our time up. Why do we wait for tomorrow to start a new project, when we have today? We do expect tomorrow will come, but what is certain is that we have today.

Today is a time for productivity, because if we don't start now, we will stall on the project and start it a year from now or we won't ever start the project at all.

This is why we have reasoning, because we can't rely on a feeling to motivate us to start a new project. Feelings come and feelings go. When we do start a project today, eventually our feelings will follow.

Goals

Today is all we have

Today is all we have. We can't think about to-morrow when we only have today. But if we do think about tomorrow, then we should plan for tomorrow.

Certainly, we have today to do what we can do to work toward our goals we've set for this year. There are 24 hours in a day.

Yes, we do have other responsibilities to take care of. We can schedule our goals between our responsibilities, but we can't blame our responsibilities for not getting our goals completed. We still have to take out the garbage and brush our teeth, but we still need to meet our goals. We just have to make our goals another part of our daily routine.

Life doesn't have to stop for us to complete our goals. But we still need to start working on our goals, since we only have today.

Have You Started Your List Yet?

If we're going to do something, we can write a to-do-list. A list makes things real, not imagined. After we write a list, we can promise ourselves to at least do one or two things off the list.

Our goal isn't to complete the list in one day, but to start it. Some of us may have a list of items that need more time while others may need a short time to complete; this is natural.

It is important to work on our list daily to keep the momentum going. Focus is also important. Having multiple projects can be overwhelming and paralyzing to a point where procrastination can set in.

If we start slow but keep at it steadily, we can eventually complete our projects. Sometimes we have deadlines to meet, but if we have an early start on our projects, then we have the opportunity to put in the time to complete them.

Be In The Trenches

When anticipating how difficult a task will be, it's harder to start and complete it. But when we start and keep our attention focused on the task at hand, there are usually no doubting or nagging thoughts about the tasks itself.

In other words, when we're in the trenches of a task, our focus is no longer on distractions but on the work. Although our goal is to complete the task, the process of the task can be rewarding.

With that kind of focus, the back of our mind is finding better ways of doing an effective job. We learn better while we're doing the task. While we're learning our way through a task, we're getting feedback on what is working and what isn't working.

Chapter 5 Doubts

Blind Spots

It's very important sometimes to listen to friends and family when we're in the state of self-doubt. When we believe we can't do something, we need a push from friends and family.

When they believe in us, it's all right to listen to them. When they see the qualities of what it takes to carry out something within us, it's all right to believe them. They have more objectivity than we do because they see what we've done over the years.

Not only do we have the blind spots in our weaknesses but we also have the blind spots in our strengths, and they see our weaknesses and strengths. We may never know what other qualities we have until someone points them out to us.

Uncertainty About Life

We all have experienced feeling uncertain about things. We want to know everything about a thing before we begin the task.

This is good to an extent but eventually we will have to move past just trying to know, because in truth we will only truly know something if we experience it.

Uncertainties are things we think might happen in the future. These are mostly in our heads and are not truly real. In fact, no one can predict the future. Wondering what's going to happen in the future is just only that—"just wondering."

After all, life is about experiencing things through our senses, like seeing the beautiful sky, enjoying an after-rain smell, and feeling and hearing the wind blowing against our bodies. Experiences like these make our hearts sing about how wonderful life is.

So Far So Good: Breaking Down Fears

"A man jumped off the top of a skyscraper. As he passed the third floor window he was heard to mutter: 'So far so good'!"[12]

When it comes to fear, we don't jump into something without having some reservations.

This example is extreme, but sometimes the feeling of fear we experience feels like we're jumping into something that causes certain death. Nevertheless, most of our fears are in our head; they aren't real.

I don't recommend that anyone jump off a skyscraper, but whatever we fear, whatever we have to jump into, we can take the attitude of the man who said, "So far so good."

This attitude can help us get through the fear, knowing that whatever the event that's increasing our fear, we can say to ourselves: "So far so good," whether it's speaking in a front of a large audience, flying in an airplane, or stepping into an elevator. The only thing that's certain is uncertainty, but we can take courage anyway.

Out of the Pit of Self-Doubt

Self-doubt can limit our choices. Without choices no one is free, and unless we widen our mind, we won't see choices that are in front of us.

Self-doubt is an obstacle we have to get through or around in life. Usually self-doubt is created when something new challenges our capabilities.

Doubt likes to occupy our thoughts when we can't think of anything else. It's difficult to find alternatives in a situation when one doubts.

How do we get out of the pit of doubts? We think of what we can do in the situation—that is, the opposite of doubt, which focuses our attention on the limitations of what we think we can't do.

Once we preoccupy our thoughts with what we can do, we feel the sensation of taking action.

Today Was Once Tomorrow

"People always have that tendency to put off working on a problem to tomorrow."
— Milton Erickson[13]

Working on a problem isn't always fun and games. When we put off working on a problem, it stays in front of us. It never leaves our sight. It hovers around the tops of our heads like flies—waiting for us to do something about it.

When a problem is dealt with, it's no longer in front us; it's behind us. We have noticed it lessen our anxiety level, we have realized that we have made the problem bigger than it actually was, and we have felt the weight of the problem lifted from us. So whatever the problem was, we got through it, since we have experienced working through it before.

Erickson is implying that the capacity in us can help us deal with the problem. Notice that Erickson says "working on a problem," not fixing or solving a problem. He wants us to begin the process of working on a problem today, thus giving our full attention to the problem today.

Today Was Once Tomorrow

If today was tomorrow and will be yesterday, then there is nothing we can do about tomorrow or yesterday, but we can do something today!

Fearing Little is the Only Way Out

"And what do you need to fear? Very little that you need to fear." — Milton Erickson[14]

Fear is a feeling. Fear saves lives. Fear is paralyzing. Fear speaks the truth about something. Fear also speaks lies. Our assumptions about a thing can fuel a fear.

Fear, if not felt, is projecting something threatening that doesn't exist. Fear is very real, but a perceived danger isn't. There are big fears and little fears. Big fears are unmanageable but– if broken down into smaller ones— manageable.

Chapter 6 Perspectives

Humor and Perspectives

Humor is good for our health. It can discharge negative energy. It helps us to deal with a difficult situation and is entertaining for mind, body and soul.

It lets us see things in a different light and stimulates the mind into thinking up new ideas. It can be a good exercise in solving problems.

Humor can lift the weight of the world off our shoulders. We can find humor in anything, if we look for it. It's good at discharging tension or breaking the ice.

It makes us laugh. It feels good in our bodies and helps support health as well as mental health. It lets us see different perspectives. Humor brings color to our world; it finds truth in everything.

Put Things In Perspective

When we're about to face some difficulties, it is time to get some perspective on them. Changing perspective helps change our attitude about the difficulties.

Asking ourselves "What am I supposed to learn from this?" can help us put things in perspective. It helps us to deal with difficulties better than if we ask ourselves "Why is this happening to me?"

So why not put things in perspective and get through them? Playing the victim game only makes things worse, not better.

Uniqueness Brings Richness To A Community

We are each unique, and although we don't always know what we want in life, we know our wants, desires, and wishes. These give us a unique perspective; no one person is ever exactly the same as another. We have the opportunity to express this uniqueness to the world.

We can all learn something from one another. Each person brings a unique perspective to the community, driven by unique desires, wants, and wishes. There is therefore a store of desires, wants, and wishes in the community to draw upon, if we so choose. So everyone brings freshness and richness to a community and we can all learn something from each other, enriching our own experience. But we can also draw from the community, a needed resource of strength.

Change Your Prototype

Milton Erickson doesn't tell his patients that they will need more flexibility; instead he sets up the patients to do something to break up the inflexibility.

Rigidity can create much anxiety in our lives. We all have rigidity, some more than others. Some of us wonder why we can't or we won't make changes that will help us in the long run.

One reason that we refuse to make changes in our lives is rigidity. Rigidity is a form of generalization.

It is because once upon a time in our earlier lives we experienced a negative event. That one negative event built a prototype in our minds, which created a generalization for future similar events. For example, a dog bites a child and thereafter the child fears every dog that he or she meets.

It's not true that all dogs the child will meet will bite. So what needs to change is the prototype of the original event.

Put A Positive Spin on A Difficult Situation

When things aren't working the way we want, we can put a positive spin on it. We can always find something positive about what we're doing.

It's easy to look at it in a negative light. Looking at things negatively just enforces the negative attitude about the situation.

But when we put a positive spin on a difficult situation, we can begin to feel less stressful and our attitude becomes positive.

As we become positive, we can better handle the difficult situation, and others around us can have an opportunity to change their attitude as well.

Visiting Loved Ones

After we have renewed ourselves visiting our loved-ones, we can take on the days ahead. Our unconscious mind is altered when we visit someone who we haven't seen for a while.

It is because each one of us brings to a gathering different points of view from different backgrounds. We're changed a little after a gathering of people.

It's interesting when we bring up what's current in the news and develop a discussion and even a little debate about them. We each have slightly different versions or more information about what's now in the news whether it's about taxes or politics.

Learning From Children?

What can we learn from children? A child likes to explore freely without limits. A child is not afraid to make a mistake when learning something new.

A child enjoys learning new things while playing. A child looks at things from a different view than an adult. Everything a child sees is from a clean slate.

Everything a child explores is new. A child enjoys listening to stories. A child enjoys touching everything with his or her hands and tasting everything with his or her tongue.

A child can do anything, as long there's a parent present to keep the child safe. Exploration and experience is a reoccurring theme that we can learn from a child.

Scientists, archeologists, anthropologists, researchers are really children in grown up bodies.

No Day is the Same

We will never repeat the same day, because each day is new.   A day is a gift.

One person may be experiencing a good day while another may be experiencing a bad day, though when we're experiencing a bad day, we can recall our good days, which helps. And while we're experiencing our good days, we can recall how well we've gotten through our bad days to get to where we are now.

Bad days give us time to focus on what really matters. Good days give us time to experience what really matters.

Staying Cool In A Chaotic World

How do we keep cool when everything around us is chaotic? We don't have to react to an event, but it's easy to do so. When our response to an unpleasant event is like a knee-jerk reaction, then the event is controlling us. Then we feel a need to control the event that we think is controlling us.

But in reality the event we are reacting to isn't controlling us; it's controlling our opinions about the event, and these are in turn causing our knee-jerk reaction.

We can take a deep breath and we can refocus when things seems to be out of our control. In this way at least, it can be helpful to change our opinions about things.

A Community of Potentials

We are a community of people, which means that, by our nature we are social creatures. We cannot survive alone; we need one another to function.

Milton Erickson often talks about human potential. We don't know how far our potentials will take us when we work together.

We're still in our infancy when it comes to our potentials. But when we look back in history, we can see how far we've come, and we can see how far we must go.

We can ask ourselves, what potentials do we have that can make a difference in our society? And, how can we work together to fulfill our potentials?

Make A Detour In Life

"It is the experience of re-associating and reorganizing his own experiential life that eventuates in a cure." — Milton Erickson[15]

We can't make a change if we're insisting on thinking of the problem the same way. We need another way of thinking, or a new frame of reference to reorganize our experiential life.

It's like taking the same route everyday to work, never considering that there are alternative routes to get to work. We're forced to take a detour only if there is problem like a car accident or road repair. But, when we do take a different route, we lose the old associations that are linked to the old route to work. The new route creates new associations and new ways of thinking, and adds varieties and new opportunities along the way.

Chapter 7 Beliefs

Sooner Is Better Than Later

"I wish I had done it sooner." This is a very common response we have after doing something that we've been putting off.

This says a lot about a belief. The main reason we put things off is because of what our beliefs or fears falsely say to us.

In spite of our limited beliefs and fears, we still have a choice of what to do. Limited beliefs or fears never take away our choices, but the beliefs and fears can make it harder to choose.

Making excuses is another distraction that delays what we want to do in our lives.

Once our decision is made, we can start working on what we wish to do in our lives. We begin to experience freedom we didn't know we had.

We're no longer prisoners of our fears and limiting beliefs. The realization hits us that we had the choice to do it all along.

Believe in the Possibilities

We need to believe in what's possible before we have a clear picture of what's possible, and for this we need to look to the past. In our experiences, we can see where we've accomplished and succeeded at things. Knowing what's possible means really looking at these accomplishments and successes and learning from them.

To put it another way, our experiences are a resource to help us see what we can do in the future. Looking into the past is useful, because when fears, doubts, and excuses are keeping us from doing what we want to do in our lives, we can always look at what we have done in our pasts that can helps us through them.

By contrast, a closed mind doesn't consider or wonder what's possible even when we see clearly what's possible for someone else. It may be that we don't want to believe something is possible for ourselves because it seems so foreign to us.

If we imagine ourselves outside looking in, only seeing the other person doing what's possible, then it feels foreign to us to consider doing it ourselves. But if we paint a picture of ourselves doing what we believe is possible, then we will have better grip on a new situation.

When We Believe In Limited Beliefs

When we live with limited beliefs, we rob ourselves of the opportunity to see how far we can go in our abilities. If we have a belief that says we can't do a certain thing, then pursuing it is out of the question.

That is, we have lost the choice to see and do what we want to do. If we have a belief that says we can't do this or that because it's too difficult, then we create a resistance to doing it.

However, we can always challenge our limited beliefs. Inner proof is more powerful than someone else trying to persuade us that we can do it. We need to test our beliefs ourselves.

You Have The Power Within To Follow Your Own Path

Our internal resource is our power to move things in our lives—resources that we have acquired over our lives through our experiences.

As long as we're gaining new experiences, we're accumulating our power. The problem for most of us is learning to get access to our resources.

Our limited frames of reference, biases, and limitations tend to get in the way of accessing resources, resources we need to follow our own path in life. When we don't follow our own path, we give our power away. Thus, following our own path can free us from bias only if we open our minds up to new ideas.

Do You Have A Purpose In What You're Doing?

Do we have a purpose for doing what we want to do in our lives? Having a purpose in what we do can give us a reason to push on during difficult times.

Some people take on a task for their family. Others are willing to go beyond the call of duty for a belief or principle that's important to them.

Having a purpose fuels our action to get things done. There will be times when we question what we are doing. Are we on the correct path? Is this worth our time?

These are questions we need honestly to ask ourselves, because finding a purpose motivates us to keep doing what is important to us.

Breaking Down Assumptions

To break down assumptions, we need to question our beliefs. Sometimes we believe things without checking them out, and when we don't check things out, we keep ourselves in the dark. But when we do question our beliefs, liberation is upon us.

We no longer have to settle for limited beliefs. Learned beliefs are passed down from one generation to the next without questioning.

We are given the answers whether we like them or not. We're not allowed to question what our parents tell us. But as adult we certainly can challenge old beliefs that are out of date in our lives.

What Is Self-Worth?

What is self-worth? Self-worth means placing emphasis on how much we value ourselves. How much we value ourselves affects every area of our lives. Self-worth can affect our relationships, it can affect our work, and it can even affect our health.

If our self-worth increases, then, these areas of our lives will be affected positively as well. Increasing our self-worth means believing and trusting in our abilities. Our capacities are there; we just need to run with them. The resources are there too; we just need to use them.

Chapter 8 Creativity

When Creativity Is Ready

It's not a good idea to force creativity; creativity is ready to show itself when we least expect it. This is why it's a good idea to carry a pen and something to write on.

Just as fast as a great idea flashes into our minds, it can disappear. We've all experienced when a great idea or solution pops into our minds that enlightens our understanding while in the midst of doing something else, then we somehow get distracted and forget what that great idea was.

The more we try to recall the idea, the more we can't remember. The good news is that our unconscious or subconscious mind will always bring up new ideas—we just have to learn how to catch them.

An Idea That Grows Into More Ideas

When we have an idea we ought not to be afraid to use it. Not every idea that pops up in our minds will be useful, but it's nice to see if it can be useful in some way.

Finding good ideas is like finding a new pair of shoes that fits; we have to try many before we find one that's comfortable. By applying an idea to a situation, we may spark another idea that fits better.

Ideas are like seeds; we just have to find the right conditions and the right climate for them to grow. A new idea helps us to expand our thinking so we can see things differently than before. Expanding our thinking helps us to look at possibilities that we haven't seen.

The Unconscious Search For Creativity

Sometimes we want an answer or an idea right away. Creativity is a wait-and-see process, not an on-demand process. When we don't have an answer or an idea right of way, perhaps we don't have a mindset to receive it yet.

When there is a delay, our unconscious minds is searching from our vast storehouse of experiences to put together ideas to help in finding a solution. The ideas usually come to us when we least expect them, usually when we are attending to other things.

Creativity, Learning and Wondering

There will always be a battle between what's revealed to us and what we don't see. Creativity is not easily given away. We must work for it. We have many questions unanswered. Creativity is a glimpse of some of those answers that we seek.

Learning the wonderment of life is entertainment. Learning is entertaining. Learning is seeking enlightenment. Life is our teacher; it's a continuous learning.

When a flash of creativity opens up our minds, we experience an exhilarating feeling of understanding that we never experienced before. Scientists, philosophers, spiritualists, and other leaders have given their lives for the quest of understanding life. It's human nature to search and wonder about life and how we play a part in the universe.

Getting It Right Is Not Always Better

As children we were free to imagine and be ourselves without any restrictions. But as we grew older our parents and our teachers told us that to master something, we had to get it right. When we began to focus on getting things right, we began losing our creativity. As result, our creativity got repressed and lay dormant inside us.

It's all right to brainstorm or to think freely without trying to get it right. When we allow ourselves to think freely, new ideas and new solutions will start to become conscious to us.

Adult thinking or conscious thinking is quick to dismiss crazy ideas or ideas that won't fit into the situation we're trying to solve. Although an idea sounds illogical, let us use our creativity to discover if the idea can find its way into solving a problem. Applying logic is one good approach, but applying creativity is even better.

A Better Way of Thinking

We don't necessarily have to think differently to solve a problem; sometimes we just need a different place to think. Changing scenery is a useful approach to help increase creative thinking. It's about rearranging our patterns, which can break up and free us from our old way of thinking. By focusing on a single idea we can stir creative thinking. If we just sit and allow ourselves to focus and attenuate all external influences, our unconscious mind will begin to take notice. Then we can just wait and see what comes up to the surface.

Expanding and More Choices

When we expand our mind, we have more choices and thus more creative freedom in our lives. Rigidity is our worse enemy.

We all have rigid biases about things. When we were young, our minds were flexible and unstructured, but as we grew older, we began to see how complicated and enormous the world was, and developed mental shortcuts to simplify things.

But now it's time for us to learn again. Expanding our minds with flexibility is like filling up a balloon with helium; it begins to rise. Our minds, like balloons, are no longer tethered by gravity; they're free and can see everything clearly, in every direction.

Chapter 9 Desires, Dreams, Drive

Creating An Inner Experience

It is within us that we create our inner experiences, and it is within us that we create change. For us to deal with reality, we must close our eyes for moment and think about our dreams and our imaginations and our learned experiences.

We are free to dream up anything we want and to do anything we want in our dreams. Our imaginations are the limit of what we can dream.

Through our dreams and our imaginations we experience many things. We have a storehouse of dreams, experiences and imaginations that are volumes of resources for us to tap into that create within us strength and courage to what we so want in our lives.

Desires, Dreams, Drive

Internal Conflicts, or Internal Peace

Having internal conflicts keeps us from doing the things we desire. Sometimes, internal conflicts are fueled by what we desire and what others desire of us.

Sometimes, we need guidance from others. It's good to listen to others and think about what we want to do in our lives.

But, the decision will always be ours to make, just as we must respect and allow others to make their own decisions.

It's a decision that we're going to live with, not the other person. We have to claim ownership for what decisions are made in our lives.

Internal conflict is very heavy on the shoulders; it's stressful on the mind and body. We can let go of the conflicts by asking ourselves, what do we want that's satisfying?

This is resolving the conflict and making peace with us. It's nice to have a mind at peace for a change.

Have You Acknowledge Your Reality

If we want to get somewhere in life, or carry out a goal, then we must acknowledge where we are now. The decisions we've made in the past directly affect us where we are today.

If we don't like where we are today, then we must make alternative decisions to those we made in our past. We cannot afford to waste time fantasizing or regretting our past decisions.

Instead, we need to use the time working towards what we need and wish in our lives. We don't have to wait till later to do something when we can do it now.

If we do something today, then we will begin to achieve some purpose in our lives.

Our desires and wants will fulfill us when we're actively pursuing them.

If we see that the floor needs sweeping and we complain how dirty the floor is, then we're lamenting. Instead of lamenting about how dirty the floor is, sweep it.

When Hope Is All We Have

Hope is a basic wish we want to fulfill. When things are turning for the worse, we grab a hold of hope, because we hope for a better outcome.

When things are beyond our control, we look for hope to guide us through trying times. Our hope begs for a little miracle to happen.

When everything has failed, hope is all we have. Hope is an expectation that something positive will come out of a difficult situation. Hope anticipates.

Hopes don't guarantee us anything, but it's all right to hope! We don't have to hope alone for something better; we can hope together, and that's powerful!

Today Is A Gift

A day is a gift to us. Receiving a new day gives us an opportunity to celebrate life. It's a good sign when someone says, "It's good to be alive." When all our senses, hearts, minds and spirits are in sync, we are experiencing a feeling of being alive.

We see the blue sky, we feel the wind blowing on our faces, and we smell everything around us.

Most of us feel most alive when we're doing some outdoor activity because our senses seem to take over.

All the outputs from our senses feed our minds and bodies. On rainy and snowy days when we're indoors, we can recall those memories to re-experience all the outdoor activities that made us feel alive.

Today is a gift because we have a new opportunity to connect with one another. Today is a gift because we have a new day to learn something worthwhile.

Listen to Reasoning and Follow your Heart

Anyone who is alive today has the stuff to bring a dream into reality. We just need to get out-of-the-way and let things happen. Either we hold ourselves back or we believe what others tell us– that it won't work.

It's okay to listen to our loved ones and friends, because they mean well, but it's also okay to listen to our hearts. Granted, we do need to hear a sounding voice to keep it real, but a sounding voice doesn't have to stifle our dreams.

We should never lose our dreams, especially when the dream is near to our hearts. It's all right to follow our hearts but it's also all right to listen to reason—a balance of both will do!

What Are Your Desires?

Do we know what we want in life, what our desires are? Have we asked ourselves what we really want in life? Sometimes, we go through life not knowing what we want or what we wish for in our lives.

Perhaps we don't give ourselves permission even to think that way. However, we do know what we don't want and what we don't desire, which lead us to the question: What *do* we want? Is that a selfish question to ask?

There are needs not met because we're not focusing on those things: we're too busy with our jobs, our loved ones, etc. It's easier to get distracted with those things than to focus on ourselves sometimes. But it's okay to sometimes be alone. If we can find the time to sit alone and close our eyes and listen to our thoughts then we might find what we really want.

Stop Dreaming, Starting Doing

We all have dreams for a better life, and we want most of our dreams to come true. Dreams alone can't make things come true in our lives; nevertheless, a dream is sometimes the only thing we can cling to, to keep us going. In fact, a dream can also make us feel good when things around us are not so good.

Eventually, we have to switch our focus from our dreams to what we can make real from our dreams.

Dreams help us push down what's negative about a situation and lift up what's possible and positive in a situation.

We need to wake up and start realizing our dreams if we think they will make us happy.

Dreams, Hopes and Fulfillments

When we dream, we're dreaming about fulfilling something in the future. Dreams help keep our hopes going; they let us imagine.

We may not have all the things we want in life but we can dream about them. Dreaming about them is motivating; it drives our hopes that these things will be fulfilled.

Our dreams and our hopes keep us going during the tough times. And it's all right to dream. In fact, we dream freely while sleeping.

In sleep, our brain can dream about various events to help discharge repressed emotions and process our thoughts; this is remarkable.

Dream It Into Reality

Let's let our dreams become a reality. We have all the resources at our disposal, if we access them. Our dreams don't have to be grand or big for them to become a reality.

Let us first start with smaller dreams; it's okay to think big, but thinking big can be over-whelming for us. Smaller dreams are much more manageable to make into reality.

It's good to start right a way, because thinking about it just delays it.

"But You Do Like Reality"

"You don't want a charming movie to end, you don't want a flower to wilt, but you do like reality." — Milton Erickson[16]

Sometimes, we like to keep our fantasies alive. In fact, some of us would rather live inside our heads. We create fantasies because we are trying to fulfill an unmet need. In the quote above, is an example of Erickson trying to return the subject, he was talking with, back to reality.

Reality is where we can get our unmet needs met, not dreams or fantasies. When we get thirsty, we don't have to fantasize about getting an ice-cold drink of water, instead we can get up and go to the kitchen and pour ourselves a glass of water.

Sometimes fantasies are useful. Consider traveling in the middle of the desert with only a short supply of water, knowing that the water has to be rationed so it will last long enough to find more water. Until we can find more water in reality, we can fantasize about drinking as much water to quench our thirst as we wish. Nevertheless, most fantasies are not like that.

Drive Through Success

Where can we find the drive to make things happen in our lives? Sometimes we need the urge to move forward to get things done.

Some of us need a deadline to get us to complete a project while others just need encouragement. Some of us love to be challenged to move forward while others would rather complete things.

Drive is what makes a successful person. But along with drive we need a clear purpose and direction. We don't want to waste our drive, because drive without purpose leads to burnout.

Our interests and motivation equals our drive to make things happen. That's what gets a successful person to look forward to getting up in the morning to do what he or she loves doing.

Move From Within

Do we know our defenses? Do we know what stops us from doing what we want to do? In psychoanalysis, a defense is a mechanism used to protect a bruised ego.

We don't like to feel exposed because there is the possibility that when we succeed in something we will get noticed. When we get noticed there is potential for criticism or attack as well as praise.

This is one of many reasons why we fear success.

But we don't have to base our motivations on external things. We can base our motivations on what drives us inside that moves us into action.

What drives us from within and where we place our attention are more important than reacting to criticisms and attacks. They can be detractors, if we're not careful.

Keep At It

Keep at it when we see no end in sight. Keep at it when everything so far has failed. Keep at it when no one but us believes in what we're doing. Keep at it when we don't see any reason to continue.

Keep at it when it's raining. Keep at it when it's snowing. Keep at it when we have a good reason to stop. Keep at it, especially, when we're in self-doubt.

Keep at it when we want to find excuses to stop. Keep at it when it seems so impossible to do. Keep at it after we have completed the task.

Keep at it when we feel tired. Keep at it when distraction is plaguing our concentration. Remember persistence is an element of success, so keep it at.

Being Centered

Sometimes we make things worse than what they are. When we get impatient, we get quick to anger. Anger is the last thing we need when we're in a situation that needs us to keep our cool.

Mistakes are easily made when we're angry because our minds become cloudy and we need our minds clear at that moment. Giving ourselves a time-out can help us to center ourselves.

Being centered helps us to make better decisions in our work or project. Anger can be useful if we channel it for injustice or protection.

Deleting Our Past

There are things in our lives we wish we could delete. It is easier to delete a word or a sentence from our computer than to delete something in our lives that we don't want to face. These issues will always come up for us. Pop psychology would call this "unfinished business."

Feelings and emotions come up and we don't know why. We have all experienced a tear flowing down our cheeks without knowing why that is. We are not thinking about anything in particular that would cause that.

A sound, a word, an image can trigger something from our past. There are things we aren't aware of or things we've forgotten about that can be a trigger.

How can we put perspective on our unfinished business? Well, the past will always be in the past; there is no turning back. But current events in our lives that trigger feelings and emotions are just indicators that we must stand back and look consciously at what those are and deal with them properly.

What Greater Joy!

"And what greater joy is there than doing what you want to do?" — Milton Erickson[17]

We all want joy in our lives. When we think back on what has made us joyful, we feel a sense of freedom that we have forgotten about; that's sometimes lacking in our present lives.

We have an adult way of thinking that restricts us from doing what we want to do as human beings. But we can allow ourselves to do what we want to do— to make us more like human beings, and less like human doings. A human doing is like a machine without feelings and emotions, but as human beings, we can see the colors of the world through our feelings.

Feel with the Finger, the Heart, and the Mind

"We do not just feel with the fingers, but with the heart, the mind." — Milton Erickson[18]

We might add to this that, since the heart is generally a metaphor of our emotions, therefore, we feel our emotions as well.

Our minds identify the emotions based on a situation or event in our world. Erickson always bring us back to basics, to experience things fully. Experiencing something different breaks up the routine of our thought processes to help in relieving repressed emotions so they can be felt fully in our heart and mind.

Don't Underestimate Your Potential

Sometimes we are so quick to criticize our work. We don't give ourselves a chance or room to grow into our potentials. We place such high standards on ourselves that we get easily frustrated with ourselves when we don't meet them.

When we get frustrated, we lose focus on what is important. What is important is learning to experience our latent potentials. Potentials are only clues and glimpses of what we can become.

Discovering our potentials can be a surprising experience. Our potentials are made from our experiences and thus help us along the way through life. And what we learned from our experiences is stored up for future uses in the guise of our potentials.

Don't Underestimate Your Potential

Chapter 10 Experiential Learning, Observation, Potential, Rigidity

When Life Teaches Us Something

It makes one wonder, why we're here living this life. Maybe we're here to learn something about life. One thing is true, we're always learning something new.

We learn to gain knowledge. We learn to experience something. We learn to better ourselves. We learn to pass on to the next generation our knowledge and experiences. Wisdom comes from years of experiencing life through our learning.

Knowledge isn't enough for us but it can be useful and helpful. Experience is a deeper way of knowing about the world and about self. Wisdom is learning something through our personal experiences.

When Reality is still Subjective

We all model reality through our background experiences.   We have different experiences; therefore, we have different realities.

No matter how real our experiences are, they're still subjective.   When we tell a story about an experience to a group of listeners, for them to understand us, the listeners have to sort through their own background to understand us.

When they do, not only are they sorting through their own experiences to understand us, but they're also experiencing the story through their background.   That's why we love to listen to stories, because we enjoy experiencing the storyteller's adventures.

A Re-Experience

In our lives each one of us has experienced something we learned that has affected our lives. It has altered the way we think: it has changed us for the rest of our lives. We sometimes return to that moment in our memory banks to re-experience it.

We want to re-experience it because it was an important moment. It probably made us change our career, or move to another state to pursue a dream opportunity to learn more about the subject.

When we are struggling through difficulties, we can look inside ourselves and re-experience that moment. That memory is like fuel that will help us get through the difficult times ahead.

Observation Brings to Life Variety

Sometimes we go through life without really looking at things. Observation can bring variety to life, because when we don't look for details, we miss out on something new. Learning something new excites us because of the self-discovery element.

We learn something interesting that we didn't know before, or we see something a little different from what we've seen before. The magic is in the details. Learning about the details take the mystery out of something.

Milton Erickson thought it was very important to experience things without analysis. When we analyze things, the experience becomes lost. But details are different from analyzing an event or something we do like walking and talking.

Learning the details is learning the 'what,' and analysis is more about learning the 'why' we do things a certain way. Observation looks for the 'what' to find new discoveries of life.

Mistakes Convert into a Wealth of Learning

"There's a wealth of learning you get from making mistakes." — Milton Erickson[19]

We have to risk doing something to make a mistake. It's okay to make mistakes as long as we can learn something from them. Learning something from a mistake means making adjustments to the situation.

If we continue to make the same mistakes, this means we haven't learned anything yet or made any adjustment to our attitude and behavior. Making adjustments mean making changes. As long as we're alive we're going to make mistakes, but also we'll have accumulated a wealth of learning—learning used as resource to breathe wisdom into a difficult situation.

Observe, then Change it

If we want to learn something about ourselves, we must observe ourselves. Most of our behaviors are done without our knowledge. If we want to make a change in a certain area in our lives we must observe what we do to resist change.

Change isn't easy. But if we want to do something to fulfill our purposes, change is a prerequisite. Change is required. That's why it's true that if we want something, it requires great labor to get it.

Change requires labor. Labor that we're not used to isn't easy. However, observing our behaviors will help us seek out those behaviors that are keeping us from doing what we need to do to make change possible.

The hardest part about change is to maintain it. It's something that we can continue to do is to keep out old habits and to maintain new changes until those new behaviors become new habits.

Time is the important element to the process of change.

Observe, then Change It

It takes time to develop new habits. Instead of waiting until tomorrow to start changing old habits, why not start today? It's just a delay if we wait for tomorrow. Remember, tomorrow is just an illusion. If we think about it, tomorrow is not real, but today is real, because we're in it.

Do We Dare to Focus On The Possibility?

If we focus on how perfect we need to be, then it would be difficult to focus on what's possible. We don't have to be perfect before we can perform on the stage of life, instead we can focus on what is possible.

What is possible, is self-evident when we reexamine what we learned over the years. The experiential learning is the gas that helps us fuel the car of life.

We just need to tap into that learning so we can trek to the different places in our lives that we haven't been before. We forget that we have a lifetime of learnings ready for us to tap into to further our lives' journeys.

Journey Loves Experiences

We all have our own journeys we trek through; no one has the same journey. On some level, we all trek through our own journeys alone.

Trekking through our own journeys alone isn't isolation from others. We trek through our own journeys together alone.

This means we each bear our own journeys, and we have made our own prior decisions to get where we are today.

Our own journeys in life are where we get our own experiences. Our own experiences are powerful resources that cannot be taken away. These resources are raw stuff that inhabits each one of us: raw stuff that is ready for use.

Life Grows In Strength

What makes us stronger is what life throws at us. Life isn't always easy; beside we would get bored if life were always easy. When confronted with life challenges, we have the opportune time for growth. Growth helps us build a foundation to handle better the next life challenge that comes our way. Each time we go through a challenge we experience growth and from growth we learn something about the experience. When the challenge is no longer in front of us, we are stronger.

Possibility

Possibility is a lovely word. Possibility means that there is a way; we just have to find how to get there. Possibility means there are obstacles we must deal with. Possibility means there is hope that we will succeed. Possibility implies potential in us that can make things happen. Possibility is like a locked door that opens—waiting for us to walk in.

Athlete with signs of Potential

"Little is really known of the actual potentials of human functioning." — Milton Erickson[20]

Milton Erickson is correct that we don't know how far we can go with our potentials. We don't know our actual potential until they are fully developed. We can't find out what those potentials are until we do something. Accumulated potentials are experiences that lie dormant until they're needed. When we hear another talk about an athlete who has potential, they're really seeing the beginning signs of potential. It will be up to the athlete to see how far he or she will go to develop his or her potential into something useful.

We shouldn't ignore these signs in ourselves, especially, when others in our world often mention these potential signs to us. Because we have the potential for something, it doesn't mean it's easy to develop it into something great. The most talented person is constantly fine-tuning his or her craft to get to a higher level.

Chapter 11 Flexibility, Freedom, Motivation, Responsibility

Craft it Out of a Routine

In other words, whatever we learn eventually becomes routine; we don't think about it anymore because it's out of our consciousness. But some routines are good, and for the most part, are satisfying enough to no longer think about improving them, like standing or walking–something we do everyday.

But there are some routines we may want to improve on, like speaking in front of a group or developing listening skills. Routines can make life dull, but if we keep improving our craft or take up something new, then it can make a difference in our lives.

Learn, Adapt, and Survive

Adaptation is learning how to make adjustments in a difficult situation. If we don't adapt we won't survive. Adapting is an attitude as well.

Optimism is one of those attitudes we must adopt, if we're going to survive. Being flexible is a keynote to adaptation. We must bend to changes in our environment.

We are one of the most adaptable creatures on the planet. We thrive to learn multiple ways to improve our lives. But we are creatures of habit and we love our routines and predictable behavioral patterns.

It's better to balance both—adaptability and routine. For a routine, we need some sort of structure, and for adaptation we need some sort of flexibility while change is happening.

When it comes to our craft or whatever we do in life, there's always room for growth. It took us a long time to learn a craft. When we're learning something new, it is usually conscious learning, and once it's learned it becomes un-conscious.

On Being Flexible

Milton Erickson was always trying to find a way to help someone be flexible. Flexibility is like a branch that's not easily broken by the wind. The branch moves in the same direction as the wind. It's like a runner who stretches before a race to prevent an injury. It's going with the flow to keep us afloat. We go with the flow and wait until things die down before we decide on the next step.

Getting Back to Riddles & Puzzles

The function of riddles and puzzles is to stretch our minds. Riddles and puzzles are a good exercise for the mind–they are not designed to give up answers easily; we have to work for them. Sometimes, we give up too soon and get upset with ourselves, only to kick ourselves after looking up the answer.

But when we do work to get the answer to a puzzle, we're rewarded with an "aha moment" —a feeling of satisfaction, a glimpse of enlightenment and understanding, a gold nugget of new perspective.

Milton Erickson enjoys using riddles and puzzles to help the subjects to expand their minds.

Seeds of Ideas

"There is nothing more delightful than planting flower seeds and not knowing what kind of flowers are going to come up."

— Milton Erickson[23]

Erickson enjoyed planting seeds of ideas to his patients, students and subjects to get them into another train of thought. This is because, when we get stuck into certain train of thought, it is hard to get out.

Confucius said, "The way out is through the door. Why is it that no one will use this exit?"[21]

Thus what seems obvious to one person isn't always obvious to another person who's thinking a certain way that's not useful. We all have experienced others pointing out to us something that seems obvious to them, and then it dawns on us what's so obvious about it. And then, we feel silly and ask ourselves, why didn't we think of that before? It's also like an "aha" moment that we get after looking for a solution. Then, when we see things in hindsight, it seems so clear.

**Flexibility, Freedom, Motivation,
Responsibility**

Bringing Down Rigidity and Uplifting Possibilities

When we bring down rigidity, we can see clearly the direction we want to go in our lives. But sometimes we frame things in such a way that we can't see the alternatives.

Then when we exercise our minds to look for alternatives, the scope of the event enlarges. When we enlarge our scope, we see the possibilities it contains.

We see possibilities that we didn't see before because of our rigid frames of reference. Possibilities were always there, we just weren't looking for them.

Once we see what's possible, we can never revert back to the rigid frames. Let us open our minds for new possibilities to our lives and rekindle and stimulate motivation to do what we're meant to.

Flexibility, Freedom, Motivation, Responsibility

Surprise, Shock, and Affirmations

Surprise is a temporary moment when our mind opens up and wants to grab hold of something meaningful before the moment of surprise disappears.

Milton Erickson uses shock and surprise with his students and his subjects to get them out of rigid mind sets. His subject is caught off guard and is looking for something to make sense of what just happened.

Erickson would say something shocking or surprising to his subjects. This awakens the unconscious mind, and then it is ready for a suggestion.

The suggestion helps break up the rigidity of the conscious mind and appeal to the unconscious mind.

So the next time we find ourselves surprised or in a shock, we can say to ourselves positive affirmations, such as "I have a vast storehouse of experiences and knowledge forged with integrity." "I am unique in every way."

Are We Normal?

What is normal? It depends on the context of the situation. We understand that it's okay to see a toddler with a temper tantrum. On the other hand, when we see an adult display a temper tantrum like a child would, then we know that's not normal. But all of us have exhibited behavior that others have questioned.

Milton Erickson defines "abnormality" as anything that falls into the class of useless behaviors. Useless behaviors are developed from the rigidity of our conscious minds that prevents our unconscious minds from using our storehouse of experiences. Experiences are our resources that we can use to aid in change.

Create Your Own Freedom

We ultimately have to choose what direction we want to go in our lives. If we dislike the present situation that we're in, then it is up to us to change it.

We have to rely on ourselves to make choices. Sometimes we don't see that we have choices, and when we feel we don't have choices, we feel like a prisoner in our situation.

When we realize that we have choices, we are free. No one can take our choices away unless we let them. Likewise, no one can create our freedom for us, because we know what's best for ourselves.

Freedom will always be linked to responsibility, and responsibility will always be linked to power. When we're free to be ourselves, then we have power and the responsibility to do things for ourselves.

Flexibility, Freedom, Motivation, Responsibility

Experiencing The New

Experiencing something new is the best way to make a change. Some things are unchanging unless we experience something that will help us change.

To experience something means actually doing something. An experience can help expand our minds so we can see that there are more choices available.

When we have more choices we have more freedom to be more of ourselves. Milton Erickson wants us to discover more about our potentials and ourselves.

He wants our minds to concentrate on the vast store of experiences that we all have and learn to use them when we need that or desire to free ourselves from the rigid ideas.

Change For Health   126

Positive Reinforcement Evokes Motivation

We all need positive reinforcement to get us to do something. Encouragement reinforces motivation. Encouragement evokes the feeling of motivation to do something.

We all need a push occasionally to get us going. Just a push is all we need to get into gear. Some of us, once we get going, can't stop, or don't want to stop.

Some of us are by nature self-motivating. Self-determination can be edifying and liberating because we aren't bound by duty; we are free to do what we want within boundaries and limitations.

Once we know these boundaries and limitations, then we can pursue our path.

Doing Our Own Thinking

It's an internal process and a powerful experience, when we're doing our own thinking. There is a feeling of freedom when listening to our own thoughts.   Erickson encourages his subjects to do their own thinking.   He gives them permission to think deliberately about their own thoughts.

From time to time, it's all right to ask for advice on something. But, after thinking it over, we still have to make the final decision and live with it. When doing our own thinking, we're asking ourselves, what do we think about this or that situation.

Doing our own thinking is a private matter; privacy gives us a sort of comfort without judgment, in listening to what we're really thinking.

When We Don't Feel Like It

We don't have to be a slave to our feelings, because feelings come, and they go. Feelings don't stick around very long.

We can't always rely on our feelings to motivate us. We know from our personal experiences that, if we wait for a feeling to motivate us, we will be waiting for a very long time.

Feelings are a product of our thoughts, or of the ideas we say to ourselves. So if we say, for instance, "Doing a certain task is difficult" then we may begin to start having a feeling of dread.

But if we replace the word 'difficult' by the word 'challenging,' then a feeling of dread is replaced by a feeling of excitement.

When we're challenged to do something, then we become intrigued and stimulated by the idea of taking action, and that alone can be motivating.

Finding Satisfaction In What We Do

Whatever we do, it's best to find satisfaction. Finding satisfaction in what we do can help us to keep quality in our work. Doing our best work increases our satisfaction.

With this satisfaction, no matter what it takes, we're willing to put in the hard work. With the feeling of satisfaction, our attention is no longer on how much we dread doing the work; instead, our attention is focused on how little time we have doing what we call our labor of love.

Finding satisfaction in what we do also means that we look forward to doing the work we care most about. The work is no longer a job but a mission with a purpose. When we focus on our mission, our time we spend on our work becomes a valuable commodity.

Things That Motivate

Milton Erickson was a master of getting his patients to do crazy things. Erickson didn't tell his patient what to do directly, instead he created an atmosphere by using the patient's unique patterns, interests and beliefs.

In so doing, he created within the person motivation to do something that could make a change. The person would begin to come up with an idea for himself to do something to make personal changes.

What the ideas, beliefs and interests are that motivate us to do something, is a question we all can ask ourselves. If we look at the things we excel in, in one area of our lives, then we probably could use the same beliefs and interests to drive us to excel in other areas.

References

1. Sidney Rosen. My Voice Will Go With You Vol. II pp. 102.
2. John Grinder, Judith DeLozier, Richard Bandler. Pattern of the Hypnotic Techniques of Milton Erickson Vol. II 1975, p. 155.
3. Ronald A Havens, Editor. The Wisdom of Milton H. Erickson. Human Behavior & Psychotherapy Vol. II pp. 32, 1985, p. 32.
4. John Grinder, Judith DeLozier, Richard Bandler. Pattern of the Hypnotic Techniques of Milton Erickson Vol. II 1975, p. 205; ver. 128.
5. Ronald A Havens, Editor. The Wisdom of Milton H. Erickson. Hypnosis & Hypnotherapy Vol. II 1985, p. 44.
6. Ronald A Havens, Editor. The Wisdom of Milton H. Erickson. Human Behavior & Psychotherapy Vol. II 1985, p. 91.
7. John Grinder, Judith DeLozier, Richard Bandler. Pattern of the Hypnotic Techniques of Milton Erickson Vol. II 1975, p. 216.
8. Statement in a press conference (1929), as quoted in Uncommon Friends: Life with Thomas Edison, Henry Ford, Harvey Firestone, Alexis Carrell & Charles Lindbergh (187) by James D. Newton, pg. 24

References

9. https://www.youtube.com/watch?v=IuY mhJUeoBE&noredirect=1

10. Ronald A Havens, Editor. The Wisdom of Milton H. Erickson. Human Behavior & Psychotherapy Vol. II 1985, p. 105.

11. Ronald A Havens, Editor. The Wisdom of Milton H. Erickson. Human Behavior & Psychotherapy Vol. II 1985, p. 143.

12. Edward deBono. Lateral Thinking. 1970, p. 36.

13. Ronald A Havens, Editor. The Wisdom of Milton H. Erickson. Human Behavior & Psychotherapy Vol. II 1985, p. 37.

14. John Grinder, Judith DeLozier, Richard Bandler. Pattern of Hypnotic Techniques of Milton Erickson Vol. II 1975, pp. 190-191, ver. 69-70.

15. Ronald A Havens, Editor. The Wisdom of Milton H. Erickson. Human Behavior & Psychotherapy Vol. II 1985, p. 124.

16. John Grinder, Judith DeLozier, Richard Bandler. Pattern of Hypnotic Techniques of Milton Erickson Vol. II 1975, p. 226.

17. Ronald A Havens, Editor. The Wisdom of Milton H. Erickson. Human Behavior & Psychotherapy Vol. II 1985, p. 32.

References

18. Ronald A Havens, Editor. The Wisdom of Milton H. Erickson. Human Behavior & Psychotherapy Vol. II 1985, p. 91.
19. Ronald A Havens, Editor. The Wisdom of Milton H. Erickson. Human Behavior & Psychotherapy Vol. II 1985, p. 45.
20. Ronald A Havens, Editor. The Wisdom of Milton H. Erickson. Human Behavior & Psychotherapy Vol. II 1985, p. 72.
21. Paul Watzlawicki, John H. Weakland, Richard Fisch. Change. Principles of Problem Formation and Problem Resolution 1974, p. 77.
22. T.S. Eliot The Sacred Wood. 1921.
23. Ronald A Havens, Editor. The Wisdom of Milton H. Erickson. Human Behavior & Psychotherapy Vol. II 1985, p. 105.

Closing Note

In closing, I would like to take this time to thank you for your interest in reading this book. I hope somehow this book has inspired you in making your dreams come true. And to know that we all have resources inside us ready to be tapped. We have potentials ready to be used to evoke inspiration and effect changes in us to live our life with the sense of freedom. Dr. Milton H. Erickson's goal was to help us to break free from what he calls our 'rigid thinking' so we can see clearly the choices that we've always had in our lives.

Also feel free to check out my website at www.changeforhealth.com where there are more inspirational messages.

M. Eugene Morgan

About the Author

M. Eugene Morgan has been an avid student of Milton Erickson's work since 1993. He received his Associates Degrees in Behavioral Sciences/ Psychology and Liberal Arts in 1994 at San Diego Community College. In 1995, he received a certificate in hypnotherapy from the American Council of Hypnotist Examiners in San Diego, CA, an interest that ties in with his interest in Dr. Erickson's work. From 1996 to1998 he has provided free hypnotherapy to clients with HIV/ AIDS at the San Diego Lesbian, Gay, Bisexual, and Transgender Community Center.

Since 1999, he has had years of exposure to the persons-served community as an administrative assistant and now as a call center representative in the Mercy Crisis Center at Mercy Behavioral Health an outpatient mental health, drug and alcohol in Pittsburgh, PA, interacting with the persons-served, therapists, nurses, doctors, and case managers. In interacting with the persons-served, he has had a great deal of success applying some of Ericksonian principles and has developed in this way a special connection with many of the persons-served over the years.